Fits of Tranquility

by

Robert Lampros

All rights reserved. No part of this book may be reproduced, stored in a retrieval system or transmitted in any form or by any means without the prior written permission of the publishers, except by a reviewer who may quote brief passages in a review to be printed in a newspaper, magazine or journal.

First printing

This publication contains the opinions and ideas of its author. JBS-- Publishing has allowed this work to remain exactly as the author intended and verbatim.

ISBN-13: 978-1512242881

Softcover

© 2015 by JBS-Publishing
Saint Louis, Missouri
www.JBS-Publishing.com

Partnered with Create Space Printing Press © 2015
CreateSpace Independent Publishing Platform, North Charleston, SC

Printed in the United States of America

For Lacey

Fits of Tranquility

Contents

Verdure	....	11
Eden	....	13
Binaries	....	14
Beautiful Night	....	15
Storms	....	16
Zephyrology	....	17
Building Character	....	18
Ninja Song	....	19
Family	....	20
The Other Side	....	21
Peace	....	22
Invisible Arms	....	23
Patience	....	24
Lightning	....	25
Reborn	....	26
Wilderness	....	27
Statuesque	....	28
Eyes	....	29
Holidays	....	30
Life	....	31
For What It's Worth	....	32
Love Scenes I	....	33
Love Scenes II	....	43

Verdure

The wind flows through the leaves
and they dance
like wings of birds threading paths
across the sky.

The grass bows beneath the touch
of its gentle hand
as it rolls uphill in giant waves
to greet us.

Plant your feet and lean against it,
you'll have a fighting chance.
Turn your back and run, who knows
where it might lead you.

Stretch out your arms, and look above
to where blue melts into pink,
where the white clouds hold fast their
royal places in the heavens.

I'm glad you found me here, on this hill.
Plants need more than air and water
to live, and sunsets don't work half as well
without beautiful eyes to watch them.

Eden

Sun, wind, and flowers
Above the dry rustling grass
A silent bird sings

Binaries

I looked up
at the sky one night,
maybe last September, and saw two
of every star. They weren't
spinning and dancing like binaries,
but only resting there,
one slightly
above the other, as if
the first had been nudged gently up,
and the dark dome of space
folded over, doubling the original,
fiery, quietly burning image
of light.

Beautiful Night

When moving is enough,
or sitting, hearing the bugs
in all the trees, watching
the birds swoop down,
as the horizon light…

You wonder, vaguely, what
morning will bring, yet know
it will be fine, and besides,
tomorrow's another world.
Your watch says 8:31.

Mosquitos now, and distant
highway rushes, fading dreams,
quiet city comforts, and rest.
And look, the stars are out now,
and the moon isn't far.

Storms

Storms don't listen
right away,
unless God's the one
speaking, and

He seems aware
that chaos
motivates the people
who stop searching.

Still, it's nice
to glimpse
Heaven, here and there,
and to know

that bad weather
on Earth
can't keep His angels
from flying.

Zephyrology

Every molecule alive, expecting
radical inversion, and free only
with regard to one another

Sink or swim, fall or fly…
breathe in, the best songs always
seem to sing themselves

Lose yourself in helping others,
and all we'll ever have to do
is glide

Building Character

Suffering brings joy,
equips us for battle—
Victory, in the myriad
firestorms of life.
Suffering gives way

To new beginnings,
launches full speed
into future riots
of heavenly color.
Suffering fades fast

Once you've decided
which side you're on,
and Who it is that
you're born to serve.
Rejoicing begins now.

Ninja Song

Forget about trying
to reassemble your mind,
when the buzzing gets
louder, there isn't much
time. Look before

Leaping, and we might
not find
all that He
promised, to
build and provide.

Up on a rooftop,
that dangerous divide,
bold speed our sole
ally, where trust
lets us fly.

Family

Outlasts everything,
because family goes
on and on, beyond
the grid of time,
space, and matter.

Starts new again,
even after crashing
waves flood houses,
and roaring winds
blast roofs bare.

Stands strong when
the trees have all
fallen, because family
takes root above
and beyond…

The Other Side

Not so much above or
below, as it is between,
streaming out from depths
ever-forward,
crying for embrace.

"Sit down," He says,
"Let Me drive," or
"Stand up, you fool,"
"Glory is waiting."
(He can say that.)

But there is a balance,
however strong or bright,
however mighty the force
rushing on, toward
or away from us.

Peace

Someday we'll wake
completely free,
our hands and feet
unbounded.

Until that time, let's
try to find
our dream beside
the fountain.

Sunlight blinds us
when we look
too high outside
the window.

Open hearts receive
harsh wounds,
while streams of life
still flow…

Invisible Arms

Breathe deeply, more than air
Surrounds you, holds you, keeps
You from every harm.

Beginning, endlessly, again
And again, passing, waking
Moments lift us brightly

Out of sight, and only
Life breaks through, where
Bruises become wings.

Patience

Always present,
alive, and calling
for us to begin
again, every day.

Slight offerings
of grace, so faint
that only a hair
could detect them.

Invisible strands
rise up into over-
reaching branches,
suddenly, in shade.

Lightning

As the world beyond
crashes in, at first
only a fracture, then
you start to wonder,
what did I do wrong?

Is that the sound
justice makes, tumbling
down the mountain?
Are those raindrops
tears of grief, or joy?

Evening fog settles
the dispute, the water
drops upon the leaves,
a sound so peaceful,
and frantic, and still.

Reborn

Water runs off
surfaces, leaving
paths of glass
disappearing and
slowly making new.

Time and matter,
with Spirit given,
return silently
abundant rewards,
as the voices of

Healing, of reason,
of Truth, speak
Light into darkness,
where death reigned,
resurrecting Life.

Wilderness

Our wilderness consists not
of sandy roots and rocks,
nor physical starvation,
nor ancient desert groaning;
visions cruel and bright.

Ours is sanded oak,
clouded steel and glass,
soufflés, Frappuccino's,
chattering voices, and un-
welcome electronic mail.

Peace in abundance,
Just around the corner,
and one more stone
to break the yoke of now.
Away, lovely friends.

Statuesque

How much more? she asks, silent, smiling.
All those ships, so much precious cargo.
These birds get their full share, so how
Much more, for you, will God provide?
Don't you know He loves us?

Waves of light greet our shore, and tread up
Over land, leaving more lights in their wake.
Life upon Life upon Life, what abundance!
A fountain rumbles, dead-center, in this place,
While half of us still dies from thirst.

Open your eyes! she cries, out there
On the water… you just can't see it yet.
Greater things than these, she says,
I'm showing you the way, don't worry.
We'll see far greater things than these.

Eyes

Your eyes don't haunt me
like two green worlds
reflecting light from dying
stars, nor like swirling
pools of silver glass, rising

Filling the skies of a new
creation, wondering
and inspiring wonder,
asking who I thought
that I could ever be.

Your eyes see my heart
instantly captured
and entrusted to you,
like two dying stars
locked in eternal orbit.

Holidays

When the universe
leans in, and
the music we hear
sings a message
of everlasting hope.

When the faces
we see, all
shine a bit brighter
with a warmth
more joyful and free.

When the light
of the world
brings life for all
people, blessing
in His great mercy.

Life

The truest breath
at last, arises
from a yearning
too broken, and
hopelessly vast.

The same breath
that gives life
carries life away,
restoring us, once
and forever.

Breathe in, awake
and keep on
changing, searching
and waiting, ever
to be free.

For What It's Worth

I've never dreamt a dream so sweet,
Or hoped to climb a cliff so steep,
Or dared to speak a sound so free,
As when I look at you.

I've never heard a voice so nice,
Or searched after a light so bright,
Or journeyed through a darker night,
Than what I have with you.

I've never trusted Jesus more,
Or cast my cares on farther shores,
Or rang the bell of Heaven's door,
For anyone but you.

You are lovely, yes, it's true,
And all I'll ever need is you,
And when I pass from this short life,
My soul will wait for you, my wife.

Love Scenes I

Dialogue

"No. No way, that's way too close to the street."

"Are you nuts?"

"Do you care if our neighbors live or not? Do you want them to die?"

"We're planting a tree."

"Yes, that's very good, honey. We are planting a tree. And if we plant it there, the neighbors will surely die."

Roger scratched his head.

"Look," said Lisa. "One, two, three, three and a half. Three and a half paces between here and the street."

"So?"

"So?"

"So what?"

"So trees grow fast, Roger, faster than you might think. It's not unrealistic to think that in two or three years this thing could—"

"Trees grow *up* faster than they grow out," he said. "What are you doing right now? What is that?"

"I'm being a tree."

Roger laughed. "You make a beautiful tree," he said.

"Thank you. Now look at my arms."

"You have beautiful arms."

"Thank you."

"For a tree."

"This is how the branches will grow. Up… and *out*…"

"Uh huh."

"Only further than that, farther than that, and in two or three years they'll be in the street. However, if we plant the tree over here a little, we'll be fine. No road obstructions, no broken glass, no screaming children, just peace."

"Good plan," said Roger. "Did you consider this?"

"What?"

"This. The walkway. Suppose someone came walking up, a UPS guy or a girl scout or someone, came walking up the driveway like–"

"You look like a girl scout."

"And they turn onto the walkway, dum-dee-dum-dee-dum, *bam!*" He clapped his hands, "Smack face-first into the branch of your brilliantly placed willow tree."

Lisa scratched her head.

"What?"

"I thought we were planting a Magnolia."

"Magnolia?"

"Like the ones in–"

"In Blue Jacket Park," he nodded, slowly.

"Yeah. Wouldn't that be nice? Right here by the walkway? Maybe not so close, right... here."

"Whatever you want, sweetheart. Anything you want, I'm game." He took a couple steps closer to her.

"Mmm-hmm, thought so. See what happens when you question me?"

Yesterday

Lunch had been decent. Smoked chicken sandwiches, steamed broccoli, cheddar cheese, and butterfly crackers. She loved butterfly crackers. He'd always thought they tasted too buttery. The field they were in was filled with tiny purple flowers—lilacs, though neither of them knew the name. She lay on her stomach with her knees bent and her feet crossed, playing lightly in the air. He lay next to her on his side, intently watching a yellow wisp of hair that was fluttering above her left ear.

"What are you thinking about?" he asked quietly. She blinked and made a sound like she would say something, but only took a breath, and let it out slowly. The breeze picked up. All the leaves and flowers began to rustle and sway.

He flipped onto his back. "It's cool how they turn like that, isn't it? The clouds... like they're curving down at us… I hope they don't eat us. Me, cloud. Me, hungry."

"Do you think about the past?" she asked him, staring out into the trees.

He squinted at her. "Sometimes. I mean, I don't avoid it."

"What do you think about?" The yellow wisp of hair kept dancing by her ear. He drew it back and fixed it.

"I don't know… who I was, where I've been, what I wanted in life, my friends… the good times."

"Only the good times?" She turned, and their eyes held together for a moment, and she looked away.

"No," he said. "The bad stuff, too. Not for long though. It's good to remember your mistakes, I think. It helps you to not make them twice."

They lay in silence for a while, him looking at her, her looking out into the trees, and the lilacs bending and rising in the wind. "I don't believe in mistakes," she said softly. The clouds swept past them overhead, slowly turning and stretching down toward them.

Today

Lisa's hair and the angle of her slightly bowed face made it difficult for Roger to see whether she was happy or sad. Besides that the sun was blazing down at them, and a metallic blue butterfly kept circling and dancing around their heads.

"I just don't understand," said Lisa.

"What's not to understand?" said Roger.

"How can you be so sure about everything?"

"Everything?"

"How can you be so sure about me?"

Roger laughed when Lisa said this. He didn't mean to laugh, not at a time like this, but given the circumstances this was the most absurd question he had ever heard. "I'm sorry," he said, and slowly he began drawing the yellow feathers of hair back from Lisa's face.

"Are you gonna answer me?"

He stopped, let his hand drop to his side. Lisa sat perfectly still, her head bowed, her face and eyes hidden. The butterfly had flown away, and around them not one leaf or blade of grass seemed to move at all. "Because you're the best one."

The words hovered there for a few seconds, then she laughed. "The best what? The best female?"

"Yes," he nodded. "You are the best female human being on this planet."

"You mean for you," Lisa added after a moment.

"Yes. Well, no. Well, in a way, yes. On the one hand," he said, "you're way too good for me. And you always will be. But on the other hand, we're made for each other. God literally made us for one another. So yes, you are the best one for me."

"Huh," said Lisa.

"Huh?" echoed Roger.

"I see."

"You see?"

"I see. Although, I do have one question."

"What's that?"

"Don't I have any say in any of this? I mean isn't free will supposed to..."

Love Scenes II

Distance

Two solid lines down the middle of the road. Two solid white lines, as far as the eye could see.

"Have you ever run this far?" he asked her.

"How far are we running?"

"Well, I don't know. If we cross the bridge and come up along the river I'd say ten, twelve miles."

"So about a half marathon?"

"Yeah, just about."

"I ran the mile every year in high school," she said.

"The one-mile?"

"Yep."

Roger shook his head.

"What?"

"Maybe we should just go fishing or something."

"What? No way. We drove all the way out here, I'm rocking these wicked new running shoes... Let's go." Lisa quit stretching and hopped over to the right side of the shoulder. "Don't feel bad when I'm back at the car and you're still on the bridge trying to catch your breath."

"Okay, don't *you* feel bad when I'm at the river and you're back at the one-mile mark." He walked up and placed his left foot even with hers on the pavement.

They turned and looked each other in the eye.

"Ready."

"Set."

"*Go!*"

Time

The car sat alone in the lot beside the lake, and they were on the roof looking up at all the stars. "I couldn't ever see it though," he was saying. "I'd always look toward the north, but I never saw the star there."

"Can you see it now?" she asked.

He glanced at the trees to the west of the lake, then over to the east where the road curved along the hillside. "There, right above the moon."

A car rolled past them, making its way up the hill. "Why couldn't you see it when you were a kid?"

Roger held Lisa's hand and drew it close to his heart. "I think you had to be here first."

Home

The stands were almost all filled at the ballpark. The vivid green seemed to shine amid the thousands of red and white hats and jerseys in the crowd. The only people on the field were the grounds crew and three umpires.

"Do you think we're going to win today?" asked Lisa.

"I think we'll win. We've got a great team this year," said Roger. "If we don't lose heart, we'll win."

The day was cloudy and a gentle breeze was moving through the stadium. "Look, even the highest rows are filling up now."

Roger looked up at the fans shuffling in to find their seats. He turned and asked her, "When you think about heaven, do you think of it as a place, like a giant castle in the sky, or is it more like a feeling, like joy or peace or love?"

She thought for a moment, and answered, "I think it's like home."

Tomorrow

The sea was calm that day. The waves drifted in to shore at an angle, breaking almost imperceptibly and gliding along the sand until fading back into the next wave, the next wave, and so on. He walked upon the golden sand, casting his gaze over the ocean, its surface a radiant blue and shimmering like a million crystals. As the sound of the waves and the light began to lift him, a face appeared with soft white skin and emerald eyes, and a mouth that spoke one word...

Made in the USA
Lexington, KY
14 June 2015